Taking the P out of Sales

An Educated Approach to Sales Success

@copyright 2024 Jeff Topp

Page 3 - Introduction

Page 8   Chapter 1: Purpose

Page 15   Chapter 2: Planning

Page 24   Chapter 3: Preparation

Page 33   Chapter 4: Personalisation

Page 42   Chapter 5: Prospecting

Page 53   Chapter 6: Persistence

Page 62   Chapter 7: Patience

Page 69   Chapter 8: Perception

Page 76   Chapter 9: Progress

Page 87   Chapter 10: Practice

Page 96   Chapter 11: Posting

Page 105   Chapter 12: Positioning

INTRODUCTION: TAKING THE P OUT OF SALES

Welcome to *Taking the P Out of Sales*. If you're here, chances are you're looking to improve your sales game, or maybe you're just getting started in the world of selling and wondering how to make a real impact. Either way, I'm glad you're here.

I've spent many years in the world of sales, not just as a salesperson but as a trainer and mentor, guiding others to find their own success. And if there's one thing I've learned along the way, it's that sales don't have to be complicated or sleazy. It's not about tricking someone into buying something they don't need. In fact, it's the opposite. The best salespeople are those who truly understand their product, their market, and—most importantly—their clients.

This book is built around a simple idea: focusing on a set of core principles, all starting with the letter "P," that will help you master the sales process in a way that's effective, authentic, and sustainable. These "P's"—Purpose, Planning, Preparation, Personalisation, Persistence, Patience, and more—are the building blocks that can turn any salesperson into a trusted advisor and consultant, the kind of person clients come to for solutions, not just for products.

Why "P's"?

Sales is full of buzzwords and jargon, but I've found that bringing it back to simple, actionable principles makes it easier to grasp.
The "P's" form a roadmap for everything from approaching a new prospect to closing the deal and building long-term relationships. Each chapter in this book is dedicated to one of these "P's", giving you a clear framework for understanding and applying these principles in your own sales process.

Why Listen to Me?

I didn't start out as a natural-born salesperson. In fact, I didn't start out in sales full stop. I used to work as a professional guitarist, songwriter, and music teacher, running my own business within the industry. But this actually taught me a wealth of transferable skills which helped shape where I am today. I also learnt first-hand how not to be sold to, having had my fair share of cold calls, dodgy sales advice and mis-sold products that were all supposed to make my business more successful. Well, they lied!

Fast forward to today, and with a wealth of knowledge and experience within sales to share, I can categorically say that the sales process has changed dramatically. The new form of sales is one of education and informed advice.

Like many of you, I had to learn the hard way—through trial and error. But what I discovered was that the key to being a good salesperson isn't about being pushy or closing deals on the first call. It's about knowing your product inside out, understanding what your client truly needs, and positioning yourself as someone they can trust.

Over the years, I've developed these methods not just to improve my own sales but to help others in their careers. I've trained people from all walks of life—whether they're new to sales, managing a side hustle, or trying to reinvigorate a stagnant business. One thing they all had in common? The need for a straightforward, no-nonsense approach to sales that actually works.

What You'll Get from This Book

This isn't your typical sales book filled with outdated techniques or flashy one-liners. Instead, it's a guide based on real-world experience, focused on actionable steps that you can start applying immediately. Each chapter will take you through a different stage of the sales process, from identifying your purpose to creating a detailed plan, from personalising your approach to staying persistent when things get tough.

You'll learn how to:

- **Define your Purpose:** Why are you selling? How do you want to be perceived? What's driving you beyond just making money?

- **Plan effectively:** A good plan doesn't just map out targets—it aligns with your purpose and keeps you focused on the right goals.
- **Prepare thoroughly:** Success in sales starts long before you speak to a client. It's about doing your homework, understanding the industry, and knowing your product so well that you can teach others about it.

- **Be Personal:** In today's sales world, personalisation is key. Clients want to feel like you understand them, not like they're just another number in your pipeline.

- **Stay Persistent, with Patience:** Not every deal will happen overnight. Sometimes, building trust takes time, but if you stay the course, the results will come.

I'm not here to give you a magic formula for instant success, because the truth is, sales takes work. But with the right mindset and a solid framework to follow, you'll find that success isn't as far off as you think.

The New Sales Process: It's About Education

One thing you'll notice throughout this book is a recurring theme: education.
The most successful salespeople I've worked with aren't the ones who push products; they're the ones who educate their clients.

They know their product inside out, understand their clients' pain points, and position themselves as trusted advisors. When you can educate your clients—showing them why your product or service is the solution they need—you've already won half the battle.

A Final Word Before We Start

Sales isn't easy, but it doesn't have to be stressful either. If you follow the principles laid out in this book, you'll be on your way to building a successful and sustainable sales career. The "**P's**" are your guide, and I'll be here with you every step of the way, sharing my own experiences and lessons learned along the way.

Let's get started.

Chapter 1: Purpose

Introduction to Purpose in Sales

Sales isn't just about closing deals or pushing products. It's about building relationships, understanding your client's needs, and positioning yourself as someone they can trust. That's why, for me, the most important starting point in sales is having a clear purpose. When you know your purpose, every sales action you take is more intentional and more effective.

Purpose gives direction not only to your sales efforts but also to how you present yourself. If you're in sales just to make money, that will show—and clients will sense it. But if your purpose is rooted in helping people, solving problems, and providing value, that shines through in every interaction.

In this chapter, we're going to explore how having a strong purpose shapes everything you do in sales. We'll also talk about how to find your purpose, how it influences your approach, and why having the right purpose is the first step to long-term success in sales.

Finding Your Sales Purpose

Before you can build a successful sales career, you need to know why you're doing it.

In my experience, salespeople who lack a clear purpose often struggle to stay motivated, and they have a harder time connecting with their clients.

Let's be honest—many people start selling because they want to make money. And that's a valid goal. But it's not enough to sustain a career, and it certainly isn't enough to build trust with your prospects. People can sense when you're in it for the money alone. They'll see you as just another salesperson pushing products, not as someone who genuinely cares about solving their problems.

I've always believed that successful salespeople are those who go beyond the transaction. They are genuinely interested in helping their clients improve their businesses or lives. That's where purpose comes in. If you're truly committed to helping your clients succeed, that purpose will guide everything you do—and your clients will notice the difference.

Ask Yourself These Questions to Define Your Purpose:

1. Why did you get into sales?

2. What do you want to achieve beyond just making money?

3. How does your product or service help people?

4. What difference do you want to make in your clients' businesses or lives?

For me, my purpose has always been about teaching others. I didn't just want to sell products—I wanted to help people become better at selling. Over the years, I realised that the best way to sell is by helping others succeed. This is what drives me to keep learning and improving, and it's the foundation for how I train others in sales.

How Purpose Shapes Your Sales Approach

When you're clear on your purpose, it affects every aspect of your sales approach. Your purpose becomes the lens through which you see your prospects, your product, and your process. It gives you the confidence to approach clients with sincerity because you know that you're offering real value.

Here's how a clear purpose can influence your sales:

1. **Building Trust**

    If your purpose is focused on genuinely helping your clients, that will come across in your interactions. Trust is a major factor in sales, and when clients feel like you're working for their benefit rather than just trying to make a sale, they're more likely to trust you.

In my own sales career, I've seen how important this is. Early on, I used to approach sales like a numbers game—making calls, sending emails, and hoping something would stick. But the results were inconsistent because I wasn't truly engaging with my prospects.

Once I shifted my focus to building trust and providing value, I started seeing a huge difference. My conversations with clients became more meaningful, and I started closing bigger, more impactful deals.

2. **Focusing on Solutions, Not Just Products**

   Purpose-driven salespeople don't just push products—they solve problems. If your purpose is rooted in helping clients, you'll naturally focus on how your product or service can meet their specific needs. Your pitch will become less about features and benefits, and more about solving real issues for your clients.

I always encourage the people I train to think beyond their product. Ask yourself: *What problem is my client facing, and how can I help them overcome it?* When you focus on solving problems, your sales conversations become more collaborative, and clients are more likely to see you as a partner, not just a vendor.

3. **Long-Term Relationships Over Quick Wins**

   When your purpose is aligned with helping clients succeed, you'll naturally prioritise building long-term relationships over making quick sales.

4. I've seen firsthand how this approach leads to bigger opportunities down the road. A client you build trust with today might come back to you in six months with a much larger deal, simply because they trust you to deliver results.

This doesn't mean you won't close deals quickly—sometimes you will. But the real goal is to establish yourself as someone clients can rely on over time. If they know you're in it for the long haul and that your purpose is to help them, they'll keep coming back to you when they need advice or support.

Purpose in Action: Examples from My Career

Let me share a couple of examples from my own career that show how having a clear purpose has made a difference in my sales success.

The Time I Almost Lost a Deal, But Saved It by Helping the Client

Some years ago, when I worked in Digital product sales, I was working on a large deal with a client in the health sector. They were interested in our product but were hesitant about the investment. In the past, I might have pushed harder for the close, but this time, I took a different approach. Instead of pushing, I focused on educating them about how our product could specifically solve a long-term problem they were facing. I provided resources, offered advice, and took the time to understand their concerns.

In the end, they didn't buy immediately—but a few months later, they came back. They had realised that what I had shared with them was valuable, and they ended up becoming a great client for me. By focusing on my purpose of helping them make the right decision rather than just closing the deal, I earned their trust and secured a long-term relationship.

Training Salespeople to Find Their Purpose

As a sales trainer, I've always encouraged people to define their own purpose in sales. One trainee of mine had been struggling with low conversion rates, and after working with him to realign his purpose, he started approaching sales with a different mindset. Instead of just focusing on making the sale, he began to see his role as helping his clients improve their processes.

Over time, he noticed a shift in the way his prospects responded to him. He started having more in-depth conversations with them, offering solutions tailored to their specific needs. His sales improved significantly because he was now selling with purpose, not just going through the motions.

Conclusion: Purpose is Your Shining Light

Having a clear purpose isn't just something that helps you start a sales career—it's what keeps you grounded throughout the process.

Your purpose is your shining light that should never burn out. When things get tough, when you face rejection or slow periods, it's your purpose that keeps you going. It reminds you why you're doing what you're doing, and it gives you the confidence to keep building trust with your clients.

As you move forward, take time to reflect on your purpose. Make sure it's something you believe in, something that drives you to offer real value to your clients. With a clear purpose, you'll find that your sales approach becomes more genuine, more impactful, and ultimately more successful.

In the next chapter, we'll look at **Planning**—how to create a roadmap that aligns with your purpose and ensures that every action you take is intentional and geared towards success.

Chapter 2: Planning

Introduction to Planning in Sales

When it comes to sales, there's an old saying: "Fail to plan, and you plan to fail." While it might sound cliché, I've found this to be true time and time again in my own career and with the salespeople I've trained. Planning isn't just about having a strategy to close deals—it's about knowing how to approach your clients, understanding their needs, and making sure every step you take is intentional.

For me, planning has always been about setting yourself up for long-term success, not just immediate wins. It's about doing the homework, creating a roadmap, and being adaptable. And most importantly, it's about having a plan that's aligned with your purpose. In this chapter, I'll walk you through how to create an actionable sales plan, why preparation is key, and how to stay flexible without losing focus.

Why Planning is Essential in Sales

Before diving into the "how," it's important to understand the "why." Sales can be unpredictable.
You can't always control when or how a prospect will respond, but you *can* control how prepared you are.

A well-thought-out plan gives you clarity and confidence. It helps you manage your time, keep track of your prospects, and stay on top of your goals.

I've worked with many salespeople who rush into selling without a plan. They make calls, send emails, and hope for the best. But without a structured approach, their results are inconsistent. Some weeks they might hit their numbers, while others they fall short. Planning eliminates the guesswork and gives you a clear path to follow.

Start with Your Purpose: Let it Drive Your Plan

In the previous chapter, we talked about the importance of having a clear purpose. Now it's time to use that purpose to guide your planning process. When your purpose is aligned with your plan, you'll find that every action you take has more meaning.

For example, if your purpose is to help small businesses become more efficient, your plan should reflect that. Your approach to prospecting, your messaging, and even the way you follow up should be tailored to that purpose. Instead of focusing on selling a product, you're focusing on showing how you can help them solve their specific problems.

My Approach:

- Before creating a sales plan, I always revisit my purpose. I ask myself: What am I trying to achieve? How can I bring value to my clients in a way that aligns with my goals? Now, you may think that this is a bit airy-fairy, but this should be something that is etched into your psyche.

- Then, I start mapping out my strategy—whether it's for the week, the month, or the quarter. Not forgetting my purpose.

Mapping Out the Sales Process: Breaking Down Your Goals

A solid sales plan has structure. It's not just about knowing who you want to reach, but also how you're going to reach them and what steps you need to take along the way. Let's break it down into practical steps:

1. **Set Clear Goals**

   It's impossible to succeed without knowing what you're aiming for. When I sit down to create a plan, I always start with clear, measurable goals. This might be revenue targets, the number of new clients, or even specific industries I want to break into. The important thing is that these goals are specific, realistic, and time-bound.

Example: If your goal is to land 10 new clients in the next quarter, break that down into weekly or monthly targets. How many prospects do you need to contact each week to hit your target? Setting these smaller milestones helps keep you on track and prevents overwhelm. *We will examine this in more detail later in the book.*

2. **Know Your Market**

Part of effective planning is understanding who you're targeting. Spend time researching your target market before making any calls or sending emails. I tend to look at industry trends, challenges that businesses are facing, and which sectors are ripe for growth. This helps me tailor my pitch and ensures I'm focusing on prospects who are more likely to need my services.

💡 **My Tip**: Don't try to be everything to everyone. Narrow your focus to a specific market or industry where your product or service can have the most impact. Then plan your outreach around that niche.

3. **Segment Your Prospects**

Not all prospects are the same, and your approach should reflect that. Segment prospects into different categories based on factors like company size, industry, or how far along they are in the buying process. This allows you to tailor your outreach and follow-up strategies to each group.

Example: You might have one segment of prospects who are in the early stages of exploring solutions. For these clients, your focus should be on educating them and providing helpful resources. For those further along in the process, you can focus on specifics like pricing and implementation.

Preparation: The Foundation of Every Good Plan

Once you've mapped out your goals and identified your target market, it's time to focus on preparation. I can't stress this enough: *preparation is everything*. I've seen too many salespeople jump into calls or meetings without doing their homework, and it almost always backfires.

When you're prepared, you're not just ready to talk about your product—you're ready to talk about how your product fits into your client's world. You know what challenges they're facing, what trends are affecting their industry, and how your solution can help.

Here's how to prepare before approaching any prospect:

- **Research the Company**: Spend time learning about the company's history, its products or services, and its position in the market. Look at their website, recent news articles, and their presence on LinkedIn. The more you know, the more credible you'll seem in your conversations.

- **Understand the Decision-Makers**: Knowing who you're speaking with is just as important as knowing about the company. Always look up your prospects on LinkedIn to get a sense of their role, their experience, and even their interests. This helps personalise the approach and build rapport more easily.

- **Prepare Questions**: Never go into a meeting or call without a list of thoughtful questions. These questions are designed to uncover the prospect's pain points and challenges. When you ask good questions, it shows that you're genuinely interested in helping them, not just selling to them.

💡 **My Tip**: Don't just focus on the product you're selling—focus on how that product can solve real problems for your client. The more prepared you are, the more valuable you'll be in the eyes of your prospect.

The Long Game: Building Relationships Over Time

One of the key lessons I've learned in sales is that success often comes from playing the long game. Rarely does a big sale happen after one meeting or phone call. Building relationships takes time, and it's your ability to consistently add value that will eventually lead to a sale.

This is where planning comes into play. I always make sure my plan includes multiple touchpoints with a prospect over time. This could be follow-up emails, check-in calls, or even sharing helpful articles or resources that I think they'll find valuable. It's not just about pushing for a close—it's about showing that you're invested in helping them, even if the sale doesn't happen right away.

My Approach:

- **Create a Follow-Up Plan**: For every prospect, I create a follow-up schedule. This might include sending a follow-up email after our first conversation, checking in two weeks later to see if they have any questions, and scheduling a meeting for a product demo after that. The key is to stay on their radar without being too pushy.

- **Provide Value at Every Step**: I never want to be the salesperson who only reaches out when they want something. Instead, I look for ways to provide value throughout the sales process. Whether it's sharing industry insights, offering advice on how to solve a problem, or just being available to answer questions, I focus on building trust.

Staying Flexible: The Importance of Adaptation

Even the best-laid plans can go off course, and that's okay. One of the most important parts of planning is staying flexible.

In sales, things don't always go as expected prospects might change their mind, budgets might shift, or market conditions might evolve. That's why I always leave room in my plan to adapt.

Here's how to stay flexible without losing sight of your goals:

- **Regularly Review and Adjust**: Make it a habit to review your sales plan regularly—at least once a month. Look at what's working, what's not, and where you need to adjust. If a certain strategy isn't yielding results, don't be afraid to pivot and try a new approach.

- **Listen to Your Prospects**: Flexibility also means listening. If a prospect gives feedback or asks for something different than what you had planned, be open to adjusting your approach. The goal is to meet their needs, not force them into your process.

- **Don't Be Afraid to Pivot**: If you find that a particular strategy isn't working—whether it's a new market you're exploring or a specific messaging approach—don't be afraid to pivot. It's better to adjust your plan than to stick with something that isn't getting results.

Conclusion: Planning for Success in Sales

Planning isn't just about setting targets or following a script. It's about being prepared, staying adaptable, and always keeping your purpose at the forefront of everything you do. A good plan gives you structure, but a great plan allows for flexibility and growth.

As you continue to build your sales strategy, remember that every action should be intentional, every interaction should add value, and every step should bring you closer to your goal.
With the right plan in place, you'll be able to approach your clients with confidence, knowing that you're prepared for success.

In the next chapter, we'll dive into **Preparation**, exploring how to thoroughly research your prospects and prepare for each interaction to maximise your chances of closing the deal.

Chapter 3: Preparation

Introduction: The Power of Preparation in Sales

Preparation is where the real work of selling begins. I've often seen salespeople focus on the final stages of the sales process—the pitch, the close, and securing the deal—without paying enough attention to the groundwork that happens beforehand. The truth is, the better you prepare, the more confident and effective you'll be when it's time to engage with your prospects.

When I talk about preparation, I'm not just referring to knowing the features and benefits of your product. It's about understanding your client's business, their pain points, their industry, and their needs—*before* you even pick up the phone or schedule that first meeting. In my experience, the salespeople who spend time preparing properly are the ones who build stronger relationships, handle objections with ease, and close bigger deals.

In this chapter, we're going to dive deep into how to prepare for success in sales. I'll share some of my personal strategies, techniques, and insights on how to prepare for every sales interaction—whether it's a cold call, an email campaign, or a face-to-face meeting. Preparation is more than just gathering information—it's about positioning yourself as someone who's done the homework, understands the client's world, and is ready to offer real solutions.

Step 1: Know Your Product Inside Out

Before you can even think about approaching a prospect, you need to make sure you know your product inside and out. This might seem obvious, but you'd be surprised at how many salespeople skip this crucial step or think they can just "wing it" during a conversation. In my years of training, one thing has become clear: if you don't fully understand what you're selling, it will show—and prospects will pick up on that.

But it's not just about memorising the features or reciting a list of benefits. Knowing your product means understanding its strengths, its limitations, and how it fits into the broader market. It means being able to explain how it works, who it's for, and how it can solve specific problems for your clients. And most importantly, it means being able to have an intelligent, engaging conversation about your product when clients start asking the tough questions.
Here's how I approach this:

- **Do Your Research**: Read every document, manual, and case study related to your product. Understand not just what it does but *how* it does it. If it's software, learn the interface. If it's a service, understand the processes involved. If you're new to the product, spend time using it yourself, if possible.

- **Know the Limitations**: Every product has limitations, and being honest about them builds trust. If your product doesn't do something your prospect needs, acknowledge it and steer the conversation towards what it *can* do. Transparency is far better than overpromising and underdelivering.

- **Be Ready for Questions**: Clients are going to ask you specific questions about your product—some that you might not expect. Be prepared for this. I always advise salespeople to practice answering questions about their product's functionality, pricing, and potential issues, so they're ready to respond confidently.

Step 2: Research Your Prospect Thoroughly

If there's one thing that will set you apart from most salespeople, it's taking the time to understand your prospect *before* you reach out. When I say "understand," I don't just mean knowing their name and job title. I mean getting to know their business, their challenges, and what's happening in their industry.

A well-prepared salesperson doesn't ask basic questions they could have easily looked up themselves. Instead, they come into the conversation already informed, ready to discuss the prospect's unique situation and how their product or service fits into it. This approach signals that you respect their time and that you've taken the initiative to learn about their needs.

Here's my method for researching prospects:

1. **Company Research:**

   Start by understanding the company's size, industry, and market position. Look up their website, recent news, press releases, and any financial reports if available. What challenges is their industry facing right now? Have they recently launched any new products, or are they going through a major shift, like a merger or expansion? This will give you context and help you tailor your approach to their specific situation.

2. **LinkedIn:**

   LinkedIn is a goldmine for research. Review your prospect's profile to learn about their career, connections, and interests. Have they written any articles or engaged in discussions relevant to their industry? This can provide great talking points for your initial conversation and help you build rapport more easily.

3. **Market and Industry Trends:**

   Go beyond the company itself—look at the broader industry trends that might affect your prospect. Is there new legislation impacting their business?

Are there economic shifts that could create opportunities or challenges for them? The more you understand the environment they're operating in, the more relevant your sales pitch will be.

Step 3: Prepare Your Personal Approach

Sales today is about personalisation. Generic, cookie-cutter approaches no longer work. When you prepare for a sales interaction, you need to think about how to tailor your message to the individual prospect, not just the company they work for. This is where your research comes into play. The more you know about your prospect's business and their personal role within it, the more targeted and relevant your approach will be.

I've seen salespeople send the same pitch to everyone, expecting it to resonate. But if you're serious about closing deals, you need to make your outreach feel like it's specifically for that client—and no one else.

Here's how I personalise my approach:

- **Start with a Personal Hook**: Use what you've learned about the prospect to open the conversation. Maybe they've recently posted an article on LinkedIn that you can reference, or perhaps their company just won an award. Mention something specific that shows you've done your homework and that you're genuinely interested in their business.

- **Speak Their Language**: Tailor your message to their industry and role. If you're selling to a financial director, your conversation will focus on Return On Investment (ROI) and cost-effectiveness. If you're talking to a marketing executive, your approach might focus on customer engagement and brand impact. Knowing the role of your prospect allows you to focus on what matters most to them.

- **Customise Your Solutions**: Based on your research, think about how your product can solve a specific issue for this prospect. Be ready to explain not just what your product does, but how it can be a solution to the exact problem they're facing. Personalising your solution is one of the most powerful ways to win over a prospect.

Step 4: Plan for Objections

No matter how well-prepared you are, objections are a natural part of the sales process. But here's the key: most objections are predictable. Clients will often have similar concerns—price, timing, or suitability of the product. The good news is that if you prepare for these objections in advance, you'll be ready to handle them confidently and effectively.

From my experience, people who are prepared for objections don't just overcome them—they use them as opportunities to build more trust with their prospects. When you're ready with thoughtful, helpful responses, it shows that you understand the prospect's concerns and have the expertise to address them.

How I Prepare for Objections:

- **List Common Objections**: I keep a list of the most common objections I've encountered within the market I am selling in, and I make sure I'm ready with responses to each one. Whether it's about pricing, product capabilities, or the competition, having these answers at the ready makes the conversation smoother.

- **Reframe the Objection**: Often, objections are just the prospect's way of expressing uncertainty. I try to reframe the objection into an opportunity to provide more information or clarify the benefits. For example, if the client says, "Your product seems too expensive," I respond with, "I understand—let me explain how our product can save you money in the long term."

- **Ask Follow-Up Questions**: When a prospect raises an objection, don't just jump into a defence of your product. Instead, ask follow-up questions to dig deeper into their concern. This helps you understand the root of the objection and allows you to address it more effectively.

Step 5: Practice and Rehearse

Preparation isn't just about gathering information—it's also about practice. The more you rehearse your pitch, your responses to objections, and your personalised approach, the more confident you'll be when it's time to interact with the client. In my training sessions, I always recommend that salespeople take the time to practice out loud, either with a colleague, family member or in front of a mirror.

This practice not only makes you more comfortable with your material but also helps you refine your delivery. The more natural and conversational you sound, the better your chances of engaging the prospect and keeping their attention.

Conclusion: Preparation as Your Competitive Edge

In sales, preparation is your competitive edge. It's what sets you apart from other salespeople who might be just winging it. When you take the time to know your product, research your prospect, and plan your approach, you come into every conversation with the confidence and knowledge you need to succeed.

Preparation isn't about perfection—it's about being ready for anything. It's about walking into every sales interaction knowing that you've done the groundwork and that you're ready to offer real solutions. So before you make that next call or send that next email, take a step back and ask yourself: Am I truly prepared to offer value to this client? If the answer is yes, then you're already ahead of the game.

Next, we'll move into **Personalisation**, where we'll explore how to make your sales process more tailored to each individual client, ensuring that every interaction feels personal, relevant, and impactful.

Chapter 4: Personalisation

Introduction: Why Personalisation Matters in Sales

In today's world, clients expect more than just a usual sales pitch. The days of sending the same generic message to every prospect and hoping for a result are long gone. Now, more than ever, personalisation is key. When you take the time to tailor your approach to each individual client, you show them that you see them as more than just a number—that you understand their unique challenges and are genuinely interested in helping them succeed.

I've learned through my own sales career that personalisation is one of the most powerful tools you can use to build trust and differentiate yourself from the competition. Prospects are bombarded with sales messages every day, and what sets you apart is how well you can demonstrate that you've done your homework and that you care about their specific needs.

In this chapter, we're going to take a look at the art of personalisation. I'll share with you the techniques I've used and taught to other salespeople that help create authentic, meaningful connections with clients. When you personalise your approach, you increase the likelihood of building long-term relationships—and long-term relationships lead to bigger, better sales results.

Step 1: Understand the Power of Personalisation

Personalisation in sales is about more than just using someone's first name in an email or knowing their job title. It's about customising your entire approach—from your initial outreach to your product recommendations—based on the specific needs, interests, and challenges of each individual client.

I've always believed that personalisation is about showing the prospect that you see them as a human being, not just as another potential sale. When I talk about personalisation, I'm talking about going deeper—about understanding the prospect's business, their role within the company, and what drives them. This kind of insight allows you to craft messages and proposals that resonate on a deeper level.

Here's why personalisation is so powerful:

- **It Builds Trust**: When clients see that you've taken the time to learn about their business and their needs, they're more likely to trust you. Trust is the foundation of any successful sales relationship.

- **It Creates Relevance**: Personalisation makes your message more relevant to the prospect. Instead of sending a one-size-fits-all pitch, you can show how your product or service directly addresses their specific problems.

- **It Shows Respect**: Personalised outreach shows that you respect the prospect's time. It demonstrates that you're not just mass emailing anyone—you're reaching out because you've identified a real need and believe you can help.

Step 2: Research Your Prospect—But Make It Personal

We touched on the importance of research in the last chapter, but when it comes to personalisation, it's about taking that research and using it to create a customised approach. The better you know your prospect, the easier it is to make your outreach feel tailored and relevant.

Here's how I personalise my research:

1. **Look Beyond the Company Website**: Yes, checking out a company's website is important, but that's just the beginning. To truly personalise your approach, you need to dig deeper. Look for interviews with key decision-makers, read blog posts or articles they've published, and follow them on LinkedIn to see what topics they're engaging with.

2. **Use LinkedIn Wisely**:
   LinkedIn is one of the best tools for personalisation. Check out your prospect's recent activity—have they commented on any posts or shared any insights?

3. **Have they attended any events or webinars**? By paying attention to these details, you can craft a message that speaks directly to their interests or recent experiences.

4. **Identify Key Challenges**:
What challenges is your prospect likely facing? Based on their industry, role, and the current market, try to anticipate what problems they might be dealing with. Once you have a sense of their challenges, you can position your product or service as the solution they need.

Step 3: Personalise Your Outreach

Once you've gathered your research, it's time to craft your outreach message. Whether it's an email, a phone call, or a LinkedIn message, the key is to make it personal and specific to the prospect.

Here's my approach to personalised outreach:

- **Open with Relevance**: Start your message by referencing something specific to the prospect. It could be a recent post they shared, an article they wrote, or an industry trend they've been discussing. This immediately signals that you've done your homework and that your message is relevant to them. DON'T open up directly talking about you or what you do!

Example: "Hi Sarah, I noticed your recent post on LinkedIn about the challenges small businesses are facing in today's market. As someone who works closely with small businesses, I understand how tough it can be to stay competitive, and I'd love to share some strategies that have helped my clients in similar situations."

- **Tailor the Value Proposition**: Don't just talk about your product's features—talk about how it specifically solves the prospect's problem. Use your research to highlight the value your product or service can bring to their unique situation.

Example: "Given your focus on improving customer retention, I think our Customer Relationship Manager (CRM) tool could help streamline your processes and give you deeper insights into customer behaviour, ultimately improving engagement and loyalty."

- **Make It Personal, Not Salesy**: Personalisation isn't just about inserting relevant details—it's also about tone. Your outreach should feel like a conversation, not a sales pitch. Keep it friendly, authentic, and focused on building a relationship.

Example: "I'd love to hear more about the challenges you're facing in this area and see if there's any way I can help. Let's grab a coffee (virtual or in person) when you have time next week."

Step 4: Customise Your Sales Presentation

Personalisation doesn't stop once you've scheduled a meeting. In fact, the most successful sales presentations are those that are tailored to the specific prospect. You've already done your research and personalised your outreach—now it's time to personalise the way you present your product or service.

When preparing for a presentation or demo, I always ask myself: *How can I make this as relevant as possible to the prospect's needs?*

Here's how I customise my presentations:

- **Focus on Their Pain Points**: Use your research to highlight the prospect's specific pain points and challenges. Make sure your presentation speaks directly to these issues and shows how your product or service can address them.

Example: "You mentioned that your biggest challenge is managing customer feedback effectively. I would be happy to show you how our tool helps centralise all feedback in one place, making it easier for your team to respond quickly and efficiently."

- **Use Relevant Case Studies**: If possible, include examples or case studies from clients in similar industries or with similar challenges. This makes it easier for the prospect to see how your solution could work for them.

- **Personalise the Solution**: Don't just give a generic overview of your product's features. Instead, customise the solution to fit the prospect's business. Talk about how specific features or services will solve their exact problems and drive results for their team.

Example: "Based on your need for better data insights, I recommend using our advanced analytics feature, which will give you real-time data on customer behaviour and allow you to make more informed decisions."

Step 5: Follow Up with Personalisation

One of the biggest mistakes salespeople make is sending generic follow-up messages after a meeting or presentation. Your follow-up is a crucial opportunity to reinforce the personal connection you've built and keep the conversation going.

Here's how I personalise my follow-up strategy:

- **Reference the Meeting**: Always reference something specific from your meeting or conversation. It could be a particular challenge the prospect mentioned, an insight they shared, or a question they asked. This shows that you were listening and that you're genuinely interested in continuing the dialogue.

Example: "Thanks again for our conversation today, Sarah. I really appreciated your insight into the challenges small businesses face when scaling their customer service operations. I've attached some additional resources that I think could be helpful as you continue to explore solutions."

- **Offer Value**: Personalised follow-up isn't just about saying thanks—it's about continuing to provide value. Send them a relevant article, a case study, or even just a thoughtful note that addresses a specific concern they raised.

- **Keep It Conversational**: Just like in your initial outreach, keep the tone friendly and conversational. Your goal is to maintain the relationship, not push for an immediate sale.

Conclusion: Personalisation as a Long-Term Strategy

Personalisation isn't a one-time effort—it's an ongoing strategy that helps you build stronger, more meaningful relationships with your clients. When you take the time to personalise your outreach, your presentation, and your follow-up, you show your prospects that you're not just another salesperson—you're someone who cares about their business and their success.

By making every interaction feel tailored to the individual client, you set yourself apart from the competition, build trust, and increase your chances of closing the deal.

In the next chapter, we'll dive into **Prospecting** —how to find opportunities and different methods of approach to a new client base.

Chapter 5: Prospecting

Introduction: The Art of Prospecting

In sales, everything starts with prospecting. It's the process of identifying potential clients, engaging with them, and building a pipeline of opportunities that will eventually convert into sales. Without effective prospecting, even the most skilled salesperson will struggle to hit their targets. But when done well, prospecting fills your pipeline with high-quality leads, giving you the best chance of success.

Throughout my career, I've learned that prospecting isn't just about reaching out to as many people as possible—it's about being strategic. You want to target the right people, in the right way, at the right time. Effective prospecting involves research, personalisation, and perseverance. It's about laying the groundwork for a relationship that leads to a sale, rather than just chasing numbers.

In this chapter, we'll dive into the strategies and techniques you can use to master prospecting. I'll share methods for identifying high-quality prospects, personalising your outreach, leveraging your existing network, working within niche markets, and building a pipeline that keeps your sales process flowing smoothly.

Step 1: Start Closer to Home—Leverage Your Existing Network

One of the most overlooked aspects of prospecting is starting with the connections you already have. Before you begin cold-calling or emailing prospects you've never met, take a look at your existing network—your friends, family, old colleagues, and current clients. Chances are, someone in your network knows someone who could benefit from your product or service. Leveraging these close connections can be a powerful way to generate warm leads.

I've always believed in the value of starting closer to home when prospecting. By reaching out to people who already know and trust you, you increase your chances of getting a positive response and a valuable referral. It's one of the simplest, yet most effective ways to start building your pipeline.

Here's how to leverage your existing network:

- **Reach Out to Friends and Family**: Your friends, family, and old colleagues might not be direct clients, but they may know people who need your services. Don't hesitate to ask for introductions or referrals—they'll often be happy to help you.

Example: "I reconnected with an old colleague who introduced me to someone in her network who needed a Customer Relationship Management (CRM) solution. That introduction led to a new client."

- **Ask Previous Clients for Referrals**: Your past clients are one of your greatest assets when it comes to prospecting. If they've had a positive experience working with you, they'll likely be happy to refer you to others. Make it a habit to ask for referrals after a successful project.

Example: "After completing a project for a client, I asked if they knew of anyone else who might benefit from my services. This led to several referrals and new business."

- **Reconnect with Old Colleagues**: Reach out to people you've worked with in the past, especially those in your industry. They may have moved on to new roles or companies where they have influence over purchasing decisions. Even if they don't need your services directly, they might be able to introduce you to someone who does.

Example: "I reached out to a former coworker who had transitioned to a management role at a new company. This led to a meeting where I was able to pitch our CRM tool to their team."

Step 2: Create a Hitlist of Local Businesses

Another effective way to jumpstart your prospecting efforts is by creating a hitlist of five businesses in your local area that you currently don't have a reach to.

These are companies that you know could benefit from your product or service but that you haven't been able to connect with yet. By focusing on local businesses, you increase your chances of finding someone within your network who knows someone at those companies, giving you a warmer introduction.

I've found that starting locally often leads to quicker wins because people are more likely to connect with someone in their community. Plus, local businesses may be more open to meeting face-to-face, which helps build trust and rapport faster.

Here's how to build and target your local hitlist:

- **Identify 20 Local Companies**: Start by identifying five businesses in your local area that fit your Ideal Customer Profile (ICP). These should be companies that you believe would benefit from your product or service but that you haven't been able to reach yet.

Example: "I identified twenty mid-sized retail companies in my area that were expanding their e-commerce operations, which made them ideal candidates for my CRM tool."

- **Ask for Local Connections**: Once you have your hitlist, start asking around. Chances are, someone in your network knows someone who works at these companies. Whether it's through LinkedIn, a local business group, or mutual friends, find a connection that can introduce you.

Example: "After creating my hitlist, I reached out to a former client who happened to know someone at one of the companies on my list. That introduction led to a meeting and eventually a sale."

- **Attend Local Networking Events**: To increase your chances of meeting people from your hitlist, attend local business networking events, chamber of commerce meetings, or industry-specific conferences. These are great opportunities to meet decision-makers face-to-face and start building relationships.

Example: "I attended a local business networking event where I met a manager from one of the companies on my hitlist. We exchanged contact information, and I followed up the next day to set up a meeting."

OR

Example 2:" I attended a local business networking event where I asked specifically for John Smith who is the head of procurement at ABC Hotel Limited"

Being specific will help to guide other in the room to know exactly who you are looking to be connected with.

Step 3: Tap Into Niche Markets Using Your Industry Experience

If you've transitioned into sales from another industry, working within a niche market where you already have expertise can be a major advantage.

Having deep knowledge of an industry allows you to "speak the same language" as your prospects, giving you an edge over competitors who might not be as familiar with the nuances of the field. Your insider knowledge helps you quickly build credibility and allows you to address specific pain points that are unique to that market.

Prospects are much more likely to engage with someone who understands their business and can offer relevant insights, rather than a salesperson who is unfamiliar with their industry. Working within a niche market where you have experience gives you a natural foot in the door and positions you as a valuable resource.

Here's how to leverage your industry experience in a niche market:

- **Leverage Your Industry Knowledge**: Use your previous experience to identify common challenges or pain points within the industry. When prospecting, position yourself as someone who understands their unique struggles and can offer tailored solutions.

Example: "I spent several years working in logistics before transitioning to sales. When prospecting logistics companies, I highlight my understanding of supply chain challenges and how my solution can help improve efficiency."

- **Speak the Industry Language**: Using the same terminology, jargon, and language as your prospects helps build rapport and shows that you truly understand their world. This can make it easier to start a conversation and establish credibility quickly.

Example: "When speaking with retail companies, I make sure to reference key terms like 'customer lifetime value' and 'omnichannel marketing' to show that I'm well-versed in their specific challenges."

- **Target Companies in Your Former Industry**: Start by targeting companies in the industry you previously worked in. You already have a deep understanding of their needs, and your connections within the industry may help you get your foot in the door.

Example: "After transitioning from the hospitality industry into sales, I focused on selling to hospitality businesses, knowing that my familiarity with their operational challenges would give me an advantage in pitching my product."

- **Use Your Network to Build Credibility**: When transitioning into a new role or industry, leveraging your existing network can help you establish credibility quickly. Reach out to former colleagues, industry contacts, and clients for referrals and introductions.

Example: "I reached out to my former boss in the logistics industry, who introduced me to key decision-makers at a company I was targeting. This helped me secure a meeting and close the deal."

Step 4: Define Your Ideal Customer Profile (ICP)

After tapping into your existing network, local connections, and niche markets, the next step is to define your **Ideal Customer Profile (ICP)** to guide your prospecting efforts. Your ICP is the blueprint for your most valuable clients—the ones who are most likely to benefit from your product or service and who have the potential to generate the greatest revenue.

When you define your ICP, you're essentially creating a filter that helps you focus on the prospects who matter most. This allows you to spend your time and energy where it counts, rather than pursuing leads that are unlikely to convert.

Here's how to define your ICP:

- **Identify Key Characteristics**: Think about the clients you've had the most success with. What do they have in common? Consider factors like company size, industry, geography, budget, and decision-maker roles. These characteristics will form the basis of your ICP.

Example: "My ideal clients are mid-sized retail businesses based in the UK, with a turnover of £5-10 million and a need for customer relationship management tools to improve their e-commerce operations."

- **Focus on Pain Points**: Your ICP should also be defined by the specific challenges your ideal clients face. What problems are they trying to solve? By focusing on prospects with pain points that align with your solution, you'll increase your chances of success.

Example: "My ideal clients are struggling to manage customer data across multiple channels, leading to inefficiencies and missed sales opportunities."

- **Refine Over Time**: As you gain more experience, refine your ICP. Review your most successful deals and look for trends. The more precise your ICP becomes, the easier it will be to target the right prospects.

Example: "After working with several retail clients, I realised that companies with a dedicated e-commerce team and a focus on customer retention are my best prospects."

Step 5: Leverage Multiple Prospecting Channels

Gone are the days when cold calling was the only way to prospect. Today, there are a wide range of channels you can use to reach potential clients, from social media and email to networking and referrals.

The key to successful prospecting is to leverage multiple channels, so you're not putting all your eggs in one basket. I've always found that a multi-channel approach leads to better results. It allows you to reach prospects in different ways and increases your chances of getting in front of the right people. Some prospects might respond to an email, while others might engage through LinkedIn or during a networking event. The more diverse your approach, the more opportunities you'll create.

Conclusion: Building a Strong Foundation Through Prospecting

Effective prospecting is the foundation of a successful sales process. It's about more than just reaching out to anyone who might be interested—it's about strategically identifying, engaging, and building relationships with prospects who are the best fit for your product or service. By leveraging your existing network, tapping into local connections, and focusing on niche markets where you have expertise, you can create a pipeline filled with high-quality leads that are more likely to convert.

Remember that prospecting is an ongoing process that requires persistence, research, and a willingness to adapt. Whether you're targeting new prospects or asking previous clients for referrals, every step you take builds momentum for future sales. Use the knowledge you have from your own industry experience, and don't be afraid to ask for help from your network to open doors to new opportunities.

Ultimately, mastering prospecting means consistently seeking out opportunities and nurturing relationships that lead to long-term success. With a well-defined Ideal Customer Profile and a multi-channel approach, you'll be well-positioned to build a healthy pipeline that keeps your sales process flowing smoothly.

CHAPTER 6: PERSISTENCE

Introduction: The Role of Persistence in Sales

In sales, persistence is often the difference between success and failure. Deals rarely close after a single call or meeting, and more often than not, it takes multiple interactions before a prospect is ready to make a decision. But there's a fine line between persistence and pestering, and finding the balance is crucial. When done right, persistence isn't about pushing harder—it's about showing up consistently, adding value at every step, and proving that you're committed to helping your client succeed.

Throughout my sales career, I've learned that persistence is one of the most important qualities a salesperson can have. But it's not just about following up for the sake of following up. True persistence is about building trust over time, nurturing relationships, and staying relevant in the minds of your prospects. Most successful salespeople I know bed themselves in for the long game. If you are looking for the quick wins, then I suggest looking at another career in the short-term!

In this chapter, I'll walk you through how to be persistent without being a nuisance. I'll share strategies for staying top of mind with your prospects, how to time your follow-ups effectively, and how to play the long game when it comes to building relationships that eventually lead to sales.

Step 1: Consistency Over Frequency

The first key to effective persistence is understanding that it's not about how often you reach out, but how consistently you provide value when you do. Bombarding your prospects with constant emails and calls is not persistence—it's annoyance. Instead, focus on delivering meaningful interactions at regular intervals. It's about showing up when it counts, rather than just being present all the time.

I've found that prospects are much more receptive to follow-ups when each interaction feels purposeful and valuable. If every time you reach out you're offering something useful—whether it's a new piece of information, a solution to a problem, or even just a thoughtful question—you're reinforcing your role as a trusted advisor, not just another salesperson trying to close a deal.

My Approach:

- **Set a Consistent Cadence**: Decide on a realistic follow-up schedule based on your prospect's timeline. For some, this might be weekly check-ins; for others, monthly updates might be more appropriate.

- **Quality Over Quantity**: Every interaction should offer value. Whether it's an industry insight, a relevant article, or a solution to a problem they've mentioned, make sure each touchpoint demonstrates that you're there to help, not just to sell.

Step 2: The Power of Value-Driven Follow-Ups

One of the most effective ways to stay persistent without being overbearing is by focusing on value-driven follow-ups. Instead of just checking in to ask if the prospect is ready to make a decision, use each follow-up as an opportunity to provide new information, insights, or support that addresses their specific challenges.

When you take this approach, your follow-ups feel less like sales pitches and more like ongoing conversations. You become someone they can rely on for useful information, and this positions you as a partner rather than just a vendor. Here's how I structure my value-driven follow-ups:

- **Send Relevant Content**: After an initial meeting or conversation, I like to send follow-up emails that include something valuable—whether it's a blog post, a case study, or an article related to the prospect's industry. This keeps the conversation going without directly pushing for a sale.

Example: "Hi Tom, I came across this article about trends in customer experience that I thought you'd find interesting based on our recent conversation. Let me know if you'd like to discuss how we can help you implement some of these strategies."

- **Provide Updates**: If your product or service has any new updates or features that might interest the prospect, share these in your follow-ups. This shows that you're keeping them in mind and that you're always looking for ways to better serve their needs.

Example: "Hi Sarah, I wanted to let you know about a new feature we've rolled out that addresses some of the challenges you mentioned around customer data management. I'd love to show you how it could benefit your team."

- **Address Their Pain Points**: If you know your prospect is struggling with a specific issue, tailor your follow-up to show how your product can help solve that problem. Even if they're not ready to buy yet, this keeps you relevant and reminds them why they initially considered your solution.

Example: "Hi John, I remember you mentioned that streamlining internal communication was a challenge for your team. I wanted to share how one of our clients tackled a similar issue using our platform."

Step 3: Timing is Everything

When it comes to persistence, timing plays a crucial role. Following up too soon can make you seem pushy, while waiting too long can cause you to fall off the prospect's radar. So how do you get the timing right?

The key is to stay engaged without overwhelming your prospect. Each follow-up should feel like a natural next step, not a forced reminder. One way I approach this is by listening carefully to cues from the prospect about their timeline, and then planning my follow-ups accordingly.

How I Manage Timing:

- **Ask for Their Timeline**: During your initial interactions, ask the prospect when it would be a good time to check back in. This gives you a sense of their buying cycle (their need) and sets expectations for future follow-ups.

Example: "I understand you're evaluating options right now. When would be a good time for me to check back in to see how things are progressing?"

- **Use Calendar Reminders**: Always set reminders in your calendar to follow up with prospects. If a prospect says they're planning to make a decision in a few months, set a reminder to check in a couple of weeks before their deadline to offer any final support.

- **Pay Attention to Their Activity**: If your prospect posts something relevant on LinkedIn or shares news about their company, use this as a natural opportunity to reconnect. This shows that you're paying attention and that you're genuinely interested in their success.

Step 4: Handling Silence with Grace

Sometimes, despite your best efforts, prospects go silent. They stop responding to emails, and your calls go unanswered. This can be frustrating, but it's important to handle this situation with. Being persistent doesn't mean you should chase them down—it means knowing when to give space and when to try re-engaging.

When a prospect goes silent, it's often because they're not ready to make a decision yet, or other priorities have taken precedence. Instead of bombarding them with messages, give them some breathing room and then try to re-engage with a fresh approach.

Here's how I handle silence:
- **Pause and Reassess**: If a prospect stops responding, I wait before following up again. After a few weeks of no contact, I reassess whether the timing is right and whether there's anything new I can offer to re-engage them.

- **Change the Approach**: Sometimes, a change in messaging can reignite the conversation. If previous follow-ups have been product-focused, I might switch to offering a free consultation or sharing new industry insights.

Example: "Hi Jane, I know things can get busy, so I wanted to check in and see if you're still exploring solutions for improving your customer support processes. I'd be happy to set up a quick call to discuss any new challenges you're facing."

- **Let Them Know You're There**: When a prospect goes silent for an extended period, I send a polite message that lets them know I'm available when they're ready but doesn't pressure them to respond immediately.

Example: "Hi Tom, I just wanted to check in one last time to see if there's anything I can do to support you in your decision-making process. Feel free to reach out whenever you're ready—I'm here to help."

Step 5: Building Long-Term Relationships

Persistence is about more than just closing the deal in the short term—it's about building long-term relationships that pay off down the road. Sometimes, a prospect isn't ready to buy today, but by staying persistent and maintaining a positive relationship, you position yourself as their go-to person when they are ready.

I've had plenty of prospects go quiet for weeks, even months, only to come back later when the timing was right. They remembered me because I stayed in touch without being pushy, and they appreciated that I was always there when they needed advice.

Here's how I focus on building long-term relationships:

- **Stay in Their Orbit**: Even if a prospect isn't ready to buy, I keep them in my network. I connect with them on LinkedIn, send occasional updates, and stay engaged with what's happening in their industry. This keeps me top of mind when they are ready to make a move.

- **Offer Help Without Expecting Immediate Returns**: I've found that offering help—without asking for anything in return—builds trust and strengthens relationships. Whether it's sharing resources, providing advice, or making a connection for them, this creates goodwill that pays off in the long term.

Example: "Hi Emily, I know we spoke about your plans for growth last year, and I just came across an event that might be helpful for you. Thought I'd pass it along!"

- **Be Genuinely Interested**: The best relationships are built on genuine interest. Ask your prospects about their business, their challenges, and their goals—even if it doesn't lead to an immediate sale. People appreciate when you take a real interest in them, and it fosters long-term loyalty.

Quick tip: If you are connecting on LinkedIn, then always connect by sending them a message or note first. You wouldn't walk down a high street and ask for contact details of everyone you meet. So be personal, introduce yourself and why you would like to connect. The beauty of LinkedIn is that you can see if your prospect has mutual connections with you. This could be useful introduction tool, as dropping the name of the mutual connection into the conversation might mean the difference to being accepted by the prospect, or not.

Conclusion: Persistence Pays Off

Persistence is about staying present without being pushy, following up with purpose, and showing your prospects that you're in it for the long haul. By providing consistent value, timing your interactions thoughtfully, and focusing on building relationships over time, you can turn prospects into clients—even

CHAPTER 7: PATIENCE

Introduction: Why Patience is a Critical Sales Skill

Patience is one of the most undervalued traits in sales. In a world where instant results and quick wins are often glorified, it can be hard to remember that the best salespeople aren't just fast closers—they're patient, consistent, and willing to play the long game. Whether it's building trust with a prospect over time, navigating long sales cycles, or waiting for the right moment to close a deal, patience is key.

I've seen firsthand how the most successful salespeople are those who understand that not every deal will happen quickly. Some prospects need time to make decisions, especially when the stakes are high. Instead of rushing the process, they nurture relationships, provide value consistently, and allow the prospect to come to their own conclusion—on their own timeline. That's where patience comes in.

In this chapter, we'll explore how patience plays a role in sales, why it's so important, and how to develop it as a skill. I'll also share strategies for staying patient when things aren't moving as quickly as you'd like, and how to manage long-term relationships without losing focus or motivation.

Step 1: Understanding the Sales Cycle

One of the first things every salesperson needs to understand is that sales cycles vary widely depending on the industry, the size of the deal, and the complexity of the product or service being sold. While some deals can close within days, others might take months—or even years. Knowing this from the outset is crucial for setting realistic expectations and avoiding frustration.

I've worked with many salespeople who feel discouraged when a deal doesn't close quickly, but the reality is that patience is built into the nature of the sales process. Long sales cycles aren't necessarily a sign that something's wrong. Often, they're a reflection of a careful, considered buying decision, especially when the investment is significant or the product is complex.

My Approach:

- **Know Your Sales Cycle**: Understand the typical sales cycle in your industry. If most deals take six months to close, set your expectations accordingly. Don't get disheartened if things are moving slower than you'd hoped—just keep nurturing the relationship.

- **Plan for the Long Term**: If you're working with a prospect who has a longer buying cycle, plan your follow-ups accordingly. Give them space to make their decision, but stay top of mind with thoughtful, value-driven interactions.

Step 2: Building Trust Over Time

Patience is closely tied to trust-building. Trust isn't something that happens overnight—it's built gradually, through consistent actions that demonstrate reliability, honesty, and genuine care for the client's needs. If you try to rush the process, you risk damaging the relationship before it's had a chance to develop.

From my own experience, I can say that the most meaningful sales relationships I've built didn't start with an immediate deal. They started with conversations, with offering advice or help without expecting anything in return, and with consistently showing up as someone who was there to support the client's goals. Over time, that trust developed into long-term partnerships.

Here's how I approach trust-building:

- **Be Transparent**: Transparency is key to building trust. If a prospect isn't ready to buy or is still evaluating options, respect that. Don't push them into making a decision before they're ready. Instead, offer to help with any questions or provide additional resources to aid in their decision-making process.

Example: "I understand that you're still considering different options, and I completely respect that. Let me know if there's anything I can do to help, whether it's answering more questions or providing additional insights."

- **Deliver Value Consistently**: Even if the prospect isn't ready to make a purchase, continue to provide value over time. This could be in the form of industry insights, helpful articles, or updates on trends that are relevant to their business. The more value you provide without pushing for a sale, the more they'll trust you.

Step 3: Managing Long-Term Relationships

Patience is particularly important when managing long-term relationships with prospects who are not yet ready to buy. It can be easy to lose focus or feel like you're wasting time when a deal seems far off, but nurturing these relationships over time is often the key to landing major deals down the road.

Some of the best clients I've worked with were prospects I nurtured for months, or even years, before they were ready to commit. They remembered me because I stayed in touch, offered consistent value, and never pressured them to make a decision before they were ready.

Here's how I manage long-term relationships:

- **Keep a Light Touch**: When managing long-term relationships, it's important not to over-communicate. Check in regularly, but don't overwhelm them with constant follow-ups. A light touch shows that you're still there, but it respects their timeline.

Example: "Just wanted to check in and see how things are going on your end. No rush on anything—I'm just here if you need anything!"

- **Be Patient, Not Pushy**: If a prospect tells you they need more time to make a decision, listen to them. Let them know you're there to support them when they're ready. The last thing you want to do is push too hard and turn them off completely.

Example: "I understand that this is a big decision, and you need time to weigh your options. I'm happy to answer any further questions you have when the time's right."

Step 4: Patience in the Follow-Up Process

Following up with prospects is one of the most important parts of the sales process, but it's also where patience is most tested. You might send an email or make a call, and then... nothing. Days go by, sometimes weeks, and you hear no response. It's tempting to keep following up, but persistence without patience can backfire.

In these situations, I've learned that patience is key. Just because a prospect doesn't respond right away doesn't mean they're not interested. They might be busy, dealing with internal issues, or simply not ready to engage yet. Instead of bombarding them with follow-ups, give them space while maintaining a presence.

My Follow-Up Strategy:

- **Respect Their Timeline**: If a prospect says they'll be ready to talk in a month, respect that. Set a reminder and follow up when the time comes, but don't rush them before they're ready.

- **Give Them Breathing Room**: If a prospect isn't responding, give them time before following up again. I typically wait a couple of weeks before sending a gentle check-in, making sure my tone is helpful, not pushy.

Step 5: The Long Game: Patience for Bigger Wins

Some of the best deals take the longest to close. It's easy to get discouraged when a prospect doesn't convert right away, but patience in sales often pays off in a big way. The relationships you nurture slowly can lead to some of the most lucrative opportunities.

You may have clients that take months—even years—to finally commit, but when they do, the payoff is normally worth the wait. They may chose to work with you because you had stayed patient, provided value, and built trust over time. These deals often turned into long-term partnerships because the relationship had a solid foundation.

Here's how I play the long game:

- **Stay in Their World**: Even if a deal is moving slowly, stay engaged with what's happening in your prospect's world. If they're active on LinkedIn, like or comment on their posts. Send occasional updates or resources that could be helpful for them. This keeps you on their radar without being intrusive.

- **Know When to Step Back**: Sometimes, patience means knowing when to step back and give the prospect time to work things out on their end. It's okay to go quiet for a while if that's what the prospect needs. Just be sure to follow up at the right time.

Conclusion: Patience Pays Off

Patience is a skill that every salesperson needs to master. It's not about sitting back and waiting—it's about staying engaged, building trust, and knowing when to push and when to give space. The best salespeople are those who understand that relationships take time, and deals don't always happen overnight. By staying patient, consistent, and focused on providing value, you set yourself up for long-term success.

In the next chapter, we'll dive into **Perception**, exploring how the way you're perceived by your clients and prospects can influence your success, and how to manage your personal and professional brand in the sales world.

CHAPTER 8: PERCEPTION

Introduction: Why Perception Matters in Sales

In sales, how you are perceived by your clients and prospects can make or break a deal. Perception is about more than just appearances—it's about trust, credibility, and positioning yourself as the expert your clients can rely on. Whether you're conscious of it or not, your clients are forming opinions about you based on how you communicate, how you present your product or service, and how you handle their needs.

I've seen talented salespeople struggle not because of a lack of skill or knowledge, but because they didn't manage their perception effectively. On the flip side, I've watched others close deals simply because they positioned themselves as trusted advisors, and their clients believed in their expertise and commitment.

In this chapter, we're going to explore how to manage perception in sales, both in terms of how you present yourself and how you create a lasting impression that builds trust. I'll share my strategies for making sure your clients see you not just as a salesperson, but as someone who genuinely understands their needs and is committed to helping them succeed.

Step 1: Managing First Impressions

First impressions matter in sales. Before you've even said a word, your prospect is already forming opinions about you based on how you look, how you've reached out, and how you present yourself. While it's not always fair to judge a book by its cover, the reality is that people do, and in sales, you want that first impression to be a positive one.

It's important to remember that first impressions go beyond just your physical appearance—they include how you communicate, your tone, and the first few things you say when you meet a client. Are you confident? Are you knowledgeable? Do you seem approachable and trustworthy?

Here's how I manage first impressions:

- **Be Prepared**: One of the easiest ways to make a great first impression is by being thoroughly prepared. When you walk into a meeting or hop on a call, show the client that you've done your homework. Know who they are, what their company does, and what challenges they're facing. This immediately sets the tone for a productive conversation.

Example: "I've been following the recent changes in your industry, and I understand that your company is focusing on expanding into new markets. I'd love to discuss how our product can support that growth."

- **Appear Professional**: Whether you're meeting in person or virtually, appearance still matters. Dress appropriately for the occasion, making sure to reflect the client's environment. For virtual meetings, ensure that your background is clean and your technology works smoothly. These small details add to your professionalism.

- **Don't Devalue Your Brand**: One of the quickest ways to undermine your perception is by not taking care of the small details. For instance, never hand over a business card with a free email domain like Hotmail or Gmail. This instantly makes your business appear less professional and less established. Invest in a branded email address that reflects your company's name—it's a small but important investment in how you are perceived.

Example: A business card that reads *johnsmith123@gmail.com* can devalue your entire pitch, as it gives the impression of a smaller, less professional operation.
A business email like *john.smith@yourcompany.com* signals that you take your business seriously.

- **Confidence is Key**: The way you speak and carry yourself also plays a huge role in how you're perceived. Clients want to work with people who are confident in what they're offering. If you believe in your product, your client will sense that. Practice your pitch so it flows naturally and be ready to answer questions with ease.

Step 2: Position Yourself as Bigger Than You Are

One of the most effective ways to manage perception is by presenting your business as larger and more established than it may actually be. This isn't about being deceptive—it's about building confidence in your ability to deliver. If you operate as a small or one-person business, using language that makes you sound like part of a team gives the impression that you have the resources and backing of a more established organisation.

This doesn't mean you should exaggerate or misrepresent your capabilities, but there are subtle ways to present yourself as a bigger operation:

- **Use "We," Not "I"**: When speaking with clients, always use "we" instead of "I." This gives the impression that you are backed by a team, even if you're running a solo operation. It helps prospects see your business as more capable and reliable, rather than thinking of you as a one-person band.

Example: Instead of saying, "I can help you with this solution," say, "We have extensive experience helping clients solve similar problems." This not only creates the perception of a larger company but also builds trust in your ability to deliver at scale.

- **Leverage Your Network**: If you work with contractors, freelancers, or partners, talk about them as part of your wider team. Positioning these relationships as part of your business can help your clients feel more comfortable, knowing that you have a range of resources at your disposal.

Example: "We work closely with our partners to ensure that every project is handled efficiently and to the highest standard."

- **Branded Materials Matter**: Ensure that all your marketing materials, from your business cards to your website, reflect professionalism. A polished brand presentation gives the impression that your business is established and credible, even if you're just getting started.

Step 3: Position Yourself as an Expert

One of the most important aspects of managing perception is positioning yourself as an expert. In sales, being seen as knowledgeable about your product or service is crucial, but it goes beyond that—you need to demonstrate expertise in your client's industry and challenges as well.

I've always told the salespeople I train: *don't just sell—educate.* When you position yourself as an expert who understands your client's world, you become more than just a salesperson; you become a trusted advisor. And clients prefer to buy from advisors they trust.

Here's how to position yourself as an expert:

- **Know Your Client's Industry**: Clients don't just want to know about your product—they want to know that you understand their industry. Stay informed about the trends, challenges, and shifts happening in their space. When you bring this kind of knowledge to the table, it shows that you're not just trying to sell them something—you're helping them navigate their industry.

Example: "I've been keeping an eye on the recent regulatory changes in your field. I think there's an opportunity for us to discuss how our service can help you stay compliant without slowing down operations."

- **Offer Insights, Not Just Information**: Clients are bombarded with information every day, but what they really want are insights. Offer a perspective they haven't thought of or help them see their challenge from a new angle. This reinforces your role as someone who brings value, not just a sales pitch.

- **Use Case Studies and Testimonials**: One of the most powerful ways to position yourself as an expert is to share real examples of how you've helped other clients solve similar problems. This not only demonstrates your expertise but also gives your prospect confidence that you can deliver.

Example: "One of our clients in the same industry was facing similar challenges with streamlining their supply chain. Let me share how we helped them achieve significant improvements in efficiency."

Conclusion: Perception as a Sales Strategy

Perception is a powerful tool in sales. From the moment you make first contact to the way you deliver your final presentation, how you're perceived influences whether clients choose to trust you. By managing small details like your business email, speaking as "we" rather than "I," and positioning yourself as an expert, you create the perception of a larger, more established, and capable company.
Remember, your goal is to build trust, confidence, and credibility with your clients. Perception isn't about pretending to be something you're not—it's about showing your clients that you're professional, capable, and ready to help them succeed.

In the next chapter, we look at **Progress**, exploring how to track your sales efforts, measure success, and continually refine your approach to achieve better results.

Chapter 9: Progress

Introduction: The Importance of Measuring Progress in Sales

Sales isn't just about landing the next deal—it's about making consistent, measurable progress. Every interaction, every follow-up, and every deal closed (or lost) is part of a broader process of learning, improving, and refining your approach. The most successful salespeople are those who continuously track their progress, understand their metrics, and adjust their strategies based on real results.

One of the biggest mistakes I see in sales is people only focusing on the end result—whether or not they closed the deal—without evaluating the steps they took along the way. This kind of all-or-nothing thinking can lead to missed opportunities for growth. By measuring your progress and setting incremental goals, you can ensure that you're improving with every interaction and moving closer to long-term success.

In this chapter, we'll explore how to effectively track your progress in sales, what metrics really matter, and how to continuously refine your approach for better results. I'll also share personal strategies I've used to evaluate my own performance, as well as the salespeople I've trained.

Step 1: Set Clear, Measurable Goals

Progress starts with having clear, measurable goals. Without specific targets, it's impossible to know if you're making meaningful progress or just spinning your wheels. But it's not enough to say, "I want to increase sales" or "I want to close more deals." You need to break those big goals down into smaller, actionable steps that you can track over time.

For me, setting goals isn't just about revenue or number of deals—it's about defining specific activities and milestones that will help me get there. It's also about being realistic and setting goals that stretch me without being overwhelming.

Here's how I approach goal-setting in sales:

- **Define Your Big Goals**: Start with your big-picture objectives. These could be things like increasing your sales by 20%, landing 10 new clients this quarter, or expanding into a new market. Make sure these goals are specific, measurable, and time-bound.

Example: Instead of saying, "I want to close more deals," try, "I want to close 5 new deals by the end of the quarter, each with a minimum value of £10,000."

- **Break Them Down**: Once you have your big goals, break them down into smaller, manageable steps. What activities do you need to do daily or weekly to reach your target? These could be things like making a certain number of calls, sending follow-up emails, or scheduling a specific number of meetings.

Example: "To close 5 new deals, I need to have meaningful conversations with at least 50 prospects this quarter. That means reaching out to 20 prospects per week."

- **Track Your Activity Metrics**: It's easy to get discouraged when you're only focused on the outcome, but by tracking your activity metrics—like the number of calls made, meetings scheduled, or demos completed—you can measure progress even before the deals close. This helps you stay motivated and focused on the actions that will lead to success.

Step 2: The 80/20 Rule—Focus on What Matters Most

One of the most powerful concepts for managing progress in sales is the **80/20 Rule**, also known as the **Pareto Principle**. The 80/20 rule states that roughly 80% of your results come from 20% of your efforts. This means that a small portion of your activities will produce the majority of your outcomes.

In sales, the 80/20 rule can apply to many aspects of your work:

- **80% of your sales come from 20% of your clients**: This means that a few key clients or deals often contribute the majority of your revenue. Identifying and focusing on these high-value clients can significantly boost your results.

- **80% of your progress comes from 20% of your efforts**: Whether it's prospecting, follow-ups, or presentations, you'll find that certain activities drive most of your progress. Understanding what those key activities are allows you to allocate your time and resources more effectively.

Applying the 80/20 rule in sales isn't about working harder—it's about working smarter. By focusing on the activities and clients that yield the biggest results, you can maximise your productivity and make faster progress toward your goals.

Here's how I apply the 80/20 rule to track progress:

- **Identify Your Top Clients**: Look at your client base and identify which clients are generating the most revenue. These are your top 20%. Prioritise nurturing these relationships and focusing on upselling or cross-selling opportunities, as they're more likely to lead to bigger results.

Example: "I realised that 80% of my revenue last year came from just 10 clients. By focusing more on these high-value clients, I was able to increase my revenue without needing to chase smaller deals."

- **Focus on High-Impact Activities**: Review your sales activities and identify which ones are driving the most progress. Are you closing more deals through follow-up calls? Is your time spent on LinkedIn generating more leads than cold emails? Focus your efforts on the 20% of activities that are driving the most results and reduce the time spent on low-impact tasks.

Example: "I noticed that my meetings with high-value prospects often led to larger deals, so I shifted my focus toward scheduling more in-depth meetings with those prospects instead of spending time on lower-priority activities."

- **Delegate or Automate the Rest**: Once you've identified your high-impact activities, look for ways to delegate or automate the less impactful 80%. This could mean using automation tools for follow-up emails or outsourcing administrative tasks so that you can focus on the activities that truly move the needle. Maybe you might need to invest some money in hiring the services of a Virtual Assistant (VA), who can then pick up some of your slack.

Step 3: Track the Right Metrics

In sales, not all metrics are created equal.
While closing deals is the ultimate goal, there are other important indicators that show whether or not you're on the right track.

I always encourage salespeople to track a range of metrics—both activity-based and result-based—so they can get a complete picture of their performance.

Here are the key metrics I track:

1. **Lead Conversion Rate**: This is the percentage of leads that turn into actual sales. Tracking your conversion rate helps you understand how effective you are at moving prospects through the sales funnel. If your conversion rate is low, it may indicate that you need to refine your pitch or improve your follow-up process.

Example: "Out of the 50 prospects I contacted, 10 have moved to the next stage in the sales process, giving me a 20% conversion rate."

2. **Average Deal Size**: Knowing the average value of each deal helps you forecast revenue more accurately. It also gives you insight into whether you're targeting the right types of clients or whether you need to focus on higher-value opportunities.

3. **Sales Cycle Length**: How long does it take you, on average, to close a deal from the moment you first contact a prospect? Tracking your sales cycle length helps you understand how efficient your process is and where there might be bottlenecks.

4. **Activity Metrics**: These are the metrics related to the actions you're taking to move prospects through the pipeline, such as the number of calls made, emails sent, meetings scheduled, or demos given. While these aren't directly tied to revenue, they give you a good sense of whether you're putting in the necessary work to hit your targets.

Example: "This week, I made 25 calls, sent 15 follow-up emails, and scheduled 3 demos."

5. **Win/Loss Ratio**: Tracking your win/loss ratio gives you insight into how many deals you're winning compared to how many you're losing. This metric helps you evaluate the effectiveness of your overall strategy and identify areas where you can improve.

Step 4: Review and Reflect Regularly

Tracking your metrics is important, but it's not enough on its own. You also need to regularly review and reflect on your performance to identify what's working, what's not, and where you can make adjustments.

I recommend setting aside time at the end of each week to review your progress. Look at your activity metrics, conversion rates, and other key metrics to see how you're performing against your goals. If you notice that you're falling short in a particular area, reflect on why that might be happening and what changes you can make to get back on track.

Here is a typical approach to a weekly review process:

- **Review Your Metrics**: Start by looking at your key metrics for the week. Did you hit your activity targets? How many leads moved forward in the sales process? How many deals closed? Reviewing these metrics will give you a snapshot of your progress.

- **Identify Patterns**: Look for patterns in your performance. Are there certain types of prospects you're consistently closing deals with? Are there specific times of the day when your outreach is most effective? Identifying these patterns helps you refine your approach.

- **Reflect on Setbacks**: If you didn't hit your goals for the week, don't be discouraged—use it as an opportunity to learn. Reflect on what went wrong and think about what you can do differently next time. Maybe you didn't follow up with enough prospects, or perhaps your pitch needs tweaking. Use these reflections to make improvements moving forward.

Step 5: Continuously Refine Your Approach

One of the most important aspects of progress in sales is the ability to continuously refine your approach based on what you've learned. Sales is a dynamic process, and what works one month might not work the next. By being flexible and open to change, you can ensure that you're always improving.

Here's a typical process to refine your sales method.

- **Adjust Based on Data**: Use the data you've gathered from tracking your metrics to make adjustments. If your conversion rate is low, you might need to refine your pitch. If your sales cycle is too long, you might need to focus on speeding up certain parts of the process.

Example: "I noticed that I'm losing momentum after the initial meeting, so I'm going to focus on following up more quickly and providing more relevant resources."

- **Test New Approaches**: Don't be afraid to experiment with new strategies. Try different approaches to prospecting, messaging, or follow-ups, and see what works best. The more you experiment, the more you'll learn about what resonates with your clients.

- **Seek Feedback**: Another way to continuously improve is by seeking feedback from your clients. After a deal closes (or even if it doesn't), ask for feedback on the sales process. Understanding how your clients perceive your approach can give you valuable insights into what's working and where you can improve.

Example: "I always ask clients for feedback after a deal closes. It helps me understand what I did well and where I could have done better."

Step 6: Celebrate Small Wins

Finally, it's important to celebrate your progress along the way. Sales can be a long, challenging process, and it's easy to get caught up in focusing on the big wins. But celebrating the small wins—like booking a meeting with a hard-to-reach prospect, closing a smaller deal, or hitting a weekly activity target—helps keep you motivated and reminds you that every step forward counts.

Here's how I celebrate small wins:

- **Acknowledge Milestones**: Whether it's hitting a certain number of calls or successfully moving a prospect to the next stage in the pipeline, take a moment to acknowledge your progress. It's a reminder that you're moving in the right direction.

- **Reflect on What You Did Well**: When you achieve a small win, take a moment to reflect on what you did well. Did you approach the prospect differently? Did you try a new follow-up strategy? Acknowledging what works helps you repeat your success in the future.

Conclusion: Progress is the Key to Long-Term Success

In sales, progress is about more than just closing deals—it's about continuously improving, learning from your experiences, and refining your approach.

By setting clear goals, tracking the right metrics, and regularly reflecting on your performance, you can ensure that you're always moving forward, even when the big wins aren't coming as quickly as you'd like.

By applying the 80/20 rule and focusing on the most impactful activities and clients, you can make your efforts more effective, maximising results while conserving time and energy. Progress isn't about perfection—it's about getting a little better every day and using your insights to drive long-term success.

CHAPTER 10: PRACTICE

Introduction: Practice is the Foundation of Sales Mastery

One of the greatest myths about sales is that success comes from natural talent or charisma alone. While those qualities can help, the truth is that mastering the art of sales is built on one key factor: practice. Whether you're perfecting your pitch, refining your negotiation skills, or learning to handle objections, the more you practice, the more confident and effective you become.

Throughout my career, I've seen that even the best salespeople didn't start out that way. They reached the top through hard work, constant improvement, and most importantly, by practicing their craft until it became second nature. Sales is no different from any other skill—whether it's sports, music, or public speaking—the more you practice, the better you get.

In this chapter, we'll explore why practice is critical for long-term sales success, how to integrate deliberate practice into your routine, and what strategies you can use to continuously sharpen your skills. I'll also share techniques I've used in my own training sessions to help salespeople improve faster and more effectively.

Step 1: Make Practice a Daily Habit

If you want to be great at anything, you have to practice consistently, and sales is no exception. Making practice a daily habit is one of the best ways to ensure that you're always improving, even when you're not actively in front of clients. Practice isn't just about role-playing sales calls; it's about sharpening every aspect of your approach—from how you research prospects to how you deliver your final pitch.

For me, practice isn't something I do now on a regular basis , but I do have to polish up my methods at times depending on the situation I find myself in. It is important to make time to refine specific elements of your sales process, whether it's reviewing your pitch, practicing how to handle objections, or studying new industry trends. By making practice a habit, you ensure that you're constantly growing and improving.

Here's a typical practice routine:

- **Set Aside Time**: Block out 15 to 30 minutes every few days to practice a specific aspect of your sales process. This could be refining your pitch, researching a new prospect, or practicing follow-up techniques. Treat it like any other important task—don't skip it.
Thinks about this process just like you would an exercise routine. The more you do it, the stronger and confident you become as a salesperson

- **Focus on One Skill at a Time**: Trying to improve everything at once can be overwhelming. Instead, pick one specific skill or area to focus on each week. This allows you to dive deep and make meaningful progress before moving on to the next challenge.

- **Rehearse Out Loud**: It's one thing to think through your pitch in your head—it's another to say it out loud. Practicing out loud helps you refine your delivery, work out any awkward phrasing, and make sure your tone is confident and natural.

Step 2: Role-Playing: Your Secret Weapon

One of the most effective forms of practice in sales is role-playing. While it can feel awkward at first, role-playing simulates real-world scenarios, giving you the chance to practice your pitch, handle objections, and work through challenging conversations in a low-stakes environment. The more you role-play, the more prepared you'll be when those scenarios arise with actual clients.

Role-playing is something I've always integrated into my sales training sessions because it allows salespeople to test their skills, get feedback, and improve in real-time. A great roleplay scenario would be to work on objections and how to handle tricky questioning from potential clients. Whether you're practicing with a colleague, a mentor, or even recording yourself, role-playing is a powerful tool for mastering the sales conversation.

Here's how to get the most out of role-playing:

- **Create Realistic Scenarios**: Don't just practice the perfect sales scenario where everything goes smoothly. Role-play difficult situations—a client with a tough objection, a price negotiation, or a prospect who isn't quite ready to commit. The more realistic the scenario, the better prepared you'll be when it happens in real life.

- **Switch Roles**: Sometimes, it helps to switch roles and act as the client. By seeing things from the prospect's perspective, you'll gain a deeper understanding of their concerns, motivations, and decision-making process. This can help you refine your messaging to better address their needs.

- **Ask for Feedback**: Whether you're role-playing with a colleague, friend, family member or recording yourself, always seek feedback. Ask for honest input on your tone, your responses, and how convincing you were. Use this feedback to fine-tune your approach.

Step 3: Practice Your Pitch Until It's Perfect

Your pitch is the foundation of your sales conversation, and it's something that should be practiced and refined continually. A strong, confident pitch can make all the difference in how a client perceives you, and it sets the tone for the rest of the conversation. But a great pitch doesn't just happen—it's crafted, practiced, and perfected over time.

Practicing a pitch is a never-ending process. Even when you feel like you've nailed it, keep refining it, adjusting for new insights, client feedback, or changes in the market. The key is to strike the right balance between sounding polished and sounding authentic.

Here's how to practice your pitch:

- **Start with a Solid Structure**: Your pitch should have a clear structure that includes an introduction, a value proposition, and a call to action. Once you have this structure in place, you can practice refining each part until it flows naturally.

Example: "Start the pitch by addressing the client's key pain point, then explain how the product solves that issue and finish with a clear next step, like scheduling a demo."

- **Personalise It**: Your pitch should never be one-size-fits-all. Practice tailoring your pitch to different types of clients or industries. The more you practice personalising your pitch, the more comfortable you'll be adjusting it on the fly in real conversations.

Example: "When pitching to a tech company, focus on how the solution integrates with their existing systems. For a small business, I'd emphasise ease of use and cost-effectiveness."

- **Record and Review**: Recording your pitch is a great way to catch any weak spots or areas that need improvement. Listen back to see how confident you sound, whether your message is clear, and if there are any awkward pauses or overused phrases.

Example: "Record your pitch once a week and listen to it critically. Ask yourself if it would convince me if I were the client, and then I make adjustments."

Step 4: Learn from Real-World Interactions

While role-playing and rehearsing are valuable, there's no substitute for learning from real-world interactions. Every client conversation, whether it results in a sale or not, is an opportunity to learn and improve. By reflecting on what went well and what didn't, you can continually refine your approach and practice new strategies.

look for areas where you could have been more effective, how did you handled objections, and whether I was able to move the conversation forward in a meaningful way.

Here's how to learn from your real-world interactions:

- **Reflect on What Worked**: After each sales call or meeting, take a few minutes to reflect on what went well. Did your pitch land effectively? Did the client respond positively to certain parts of the conversation? Reflecting on what worked allows you to replicate those successes in future interactions.

Example: "I noticed that when I asked more open-ended questions, the client was more engaged. I made a note to incorporate more of those types of questions in future calls."

- **Identify Areas for Improvement**: Equally important is identifying areas where you could have done better. Maybe you missed an opportunity to address a key objection, or perhaps you rushed through your pitch. Use these reflections as opportunities for growth.

Example: "In a recent call, I realised I didn't ask enough questions to fully understand the client's needs. Next time, I'll focus on listening more before offering solutions."

- **Ask for Feedback from Clients**: Sometimes, the best feedback comes directly from your clients. Don't be afraid to ask them how they felt about the conversation, especially if you have a good rapport. Their input can help you understand what resonated with them and where you can improve.

Step 5: Practice Resilience

In sales, rejection is inevitable. Not every prospect will say yes, and not every deal will close. But the key to long-term success is resilience—the ability to bounce back from rejection and keep going. Practicing resilience is just as important as practicing your pitch because it helps you stay motivated and focused, even when things don't go as planned.

I've faced my fair share of rejections, but I've learned that every "no" is an opportunity to learn and improve. The more you practice resilience, the easier it becomes to handle setbacks and turn them into stepping stones toward future success.

Here's how to practice resilience:

- **Don't Take Rejection Personally**: It's easy to feel discouraged when a deal doesn't go your way, but remember that rejection is a natural part of sales. Instead of taking it personally, view it as a chance to reflect on what you can improve.

- **Bounce Back Quickly**: The faster you can move on from a rejection, the better. After reflecting on what went wrong, shift your focus back to your next opportunity. Staying positive and forward-thinking is key to maintaining momentum.

- **Celebrate the Effort**: Even if a deal doesn't close, celebrate the effort you put in. Recognise that every interaction, even the ones that don't go your way, is part of the process of getting better. By staying resilient, you'll improve your skills and increase your chances of success in the long run.

Conclusion: Practice Makes Perfect

In sales, mastery comes from constant practice. It's not about being perfect from day one—it's about continually honing your skills, learning from your experiences, and refining your approach. Whether you're practicing your pitch, role-playing difficult scenarios, or reflecting on real-world interactions, every bit of practice brings you one step closer to becoming the best salesperson you can be.

By making practice a daily habit, seeking feedback, and building resilience, you'll not only improve your skills but also gain the confidence needed to navigate any sales situation with ease.

In the next chapter, we'll focus on **Posting**, where we'll explore how to use social media effectively to build credibility, engage with prospects, and position yourself as an expert in your field.

Chapter 11: Posting

Introduction: The Power of Posting in Sales

In today's digital world, social media is one of the most powerful tools at your disposal as a salesperson. It's no longer enough to simply rely on cold calls and emails—your prospects are spending time online, researching, learning, and connecting. Posting regularly on platforms like LinkedIn and other social media platforms allows you to engage with these prospects in a non-intrusive way, building credibility and positioning yourself as an expert in your field.

But effective posting is more than just broadcasting information. It's about fostering conversations, sharing insights, and showing that you understand your industry and your clients' needs. If done right, posting can open the door to meaningful interactions and create opportunities for your prospects to approach you, rather than the other way around.

In this chapter, we'll explore how to make the most of posting on social media, especially LinkedIn. I'll show you how to create content that resonates with your audience, how to engage with others to build relationships, and how to use posting as a strategic tool for driving sales.

Step 1: Define Your Goals and Audience

Before you start posting on social media, it's important to be clear about your goals and who you're trying to reach. Are you trying to establish yourself as a thought leader in your industry? Are you looking to generate leads and attract new prospects? Or are you simply trying to stay top of mind with your existing network?

Once you've defined your goals, the next step is to think about your audience. Who are you trying to connect with? Are they decision-makers, business owners, or industry professionals? Understanding your audience helps you tailor your content to their specific needs and interests.

Here's how to get started:

- **Set Clear Goals**: Think about what you want to achieve with your posts. Are you trying to build credibility, generate leads, or engage with existing clients? Having clear goals will help you create more focused and effective content.

Example: "I want to position myself as a CRM expert, offering valuable tips and insights to small business owners looking to improve customer engagement."

- **Identify Your Target Audience**: Who are your ideal clients? What industries are they in, and what challenges are they facing? Knowing your audience helps you create content that resonates with them and adds value to their specific situation.

Example: "I'm targeting small business owners and sales managers who are looking for practical ways to streamline their sales processes."

Step 2: Share Valuable, Relevant Content

Once you know your goals and audience, it's time to start posting content that adds value. The key to effective posting is to focus on quality over quantity. Your content should be informative, insightful, and relevant to your audience's needs. The more value you provide, the more likely prospects are to engage with you, follow your updates, and ultimately see you as a trusted resource.

When I post on LinkedIn, I always ask myself: *Is this useful for my audience? Does this help them solve a problem or think about something in a new way?* By focusing on adding value, you build credibility and trust, which is essential for driving sales.

Here's what to post:

- **Industry Insights**: Share your knowledge of industry trends, challenges, and opportunities. Position yourself as someone who stays on top of the latest developments and can offer valuable perspectives.

Example: "With recent changes in data privacy regulations, small businesses need to rethink how they manage customer data. Here are three strategies to ensure compliance while maintaining efficient customer service."

- **Practical Tips and How-To's**: Your audience is likely looking for actionable advice that can help them solve problems. Share tips, strategies, or how-to guides that they can implement in their businesses.

Example: "Struggling to keep track of client interactions? Here are five ways to optimise your CRM system to boost customer retention."

- **Case Studies and Success Stories**: Sharing real-world examples of how you've helped clients succeed is a powerful way to demonstrate your expertise. Highlight the challenges your client faced, how you helped them, and the results they achieved.

Example: "One of my clients increased their sales by 25% after streamlining their CRM processes. Here's how we worked together to achieve that result."

- **Ask Questions**: Social media is about engagement, not just broadcasting. Asking open-ended questions encourages your audience to interact with you, creating conversations that can lead to new opportunities.

Example: "What's the biggest challenge you're facing with your CRM system right now? Let's discuss solutions that could help."

Step 3: Engage with Others—It's Not Just About Posting

While posting content is important, social media is a two-way street. Engagement is just as crucial as creating posts. By interacting with others—commenting on their posts, sharing their insights, and joining relevant conversations—you can build relationships and increase your visibility in your industry.

I've found that engaging with others' content can often be more effective than simply posting my own. When you comment thoughtfully on someone's post or share an interesting article with your perspective, you're demonstrating that you're not just there to talk—you're there to listen and contribute to the conversation.

Here's how to engage effectively:

- **Comment on Posts**: When you see a post that resonates with you, take the time to leave a thoughtful comment. Share your insights, ask a follow-up question, or offer additional advice. This helps you connect with the original poster and shows others that you're engaged and knowledgeable.

Example: "Great point about customer retention strategies! I've found that focusing on personalising customer follow-ups can make a huge difference. What has been your experience with that?"

- **Like and Share**: Liking and sharing relevant posts is a simple way to stay active and visible on social media. When you share content, add your own perspective or comment to provide value to your network, as well as placing your comment in front of the post owner's audience and connections.

Example: "This article on the future of CRM is a must-read for anyone in sales. I especially agree with the point about automating follow-ups to save time and improve customer satisfaction."

- **Join Groups and Conversations**: LinkedIn groups and industry discussions are great places to connect with like-minded professionals. By contributing to these conversations, you can expand your network and demonstrate your expertise in a more focused environment.

Example: "I regularly participate in CRM industry groups where I share tips and discuss trends with other professionals. This has led to some valuable connections and new opportunities."

Step 4: Be Consistent and Strategic

Consistency is key when it comes to posting on social media. It's not enough to post once in a while—you need to stay active to remain visible and relevant. However, consistency doesn't mean you should post for the sake of posting. Every post should have a purpose and add value to your audience.

For me, being strategic about posting means planning my content in advance and ensuring that each post aligns with my goals. Whether I'm trying to engage prospects, educate my network, or showcase my expertise, I make sure that every post serves a clear purpose.

Here's how to stay consistent and strategic:

- **Create a Posting Schedule**: Decide how often you want to post and stick to a schedule. Whether it's once a day or a few times a week, consistency helps keep you top of mind with your audience.

Example: "I aim to post on LinkedIn three times a week— one post focused on industry trends, one on client success stories, and one with actionable tips for my audience."

- **Use a Content Calendar**: Planning your content in advance can help ensure that you're posting a variety of valuable content. A content calendar allows you to map out your posts for the week or month, so you're not scrambling for ideas at the last minute.

Example: "I plan my content at the start of each month, ensuring I have a good mix of educational posts, client stories, and engagement-focused questions."

- **Mix Up Your Content**: Don't post the same type of content every time. Mix it up with a combination of articles, videos, infographics, and questions. This keeps your audience engaged and interested in what you have to say.

Step 5: Track Engagement and Refine Your Strategy

Just like any other aspect of sales, it's important to track your progress and refine your strategy over time. Pay attention to which posts generate the most engagement—likes, comments, shares—and use this information to adjust your content strategy. If certain types of posts consistently perform well, consider posting more of that content. If some posts fall flat, figure out why and adjust accordingly.

I always review my social media performance at the end of each month, looking at which posts generated the most interest and how many new connections or conversations were sparked. This helps me refine my strategy and ensure that my posts are resonating with my audience.

Here's how to track and refine your posting strategy:

- **Monitor Engagement Metrics**: Pay attention to likes, comments, and shares on your posts. Which posts are getting the most engagement? Which ones are sparking conversations? Use this data to guide future content.

Example: "I noticed that my posts offering practical CRM tips consistently get the most engagement, so I've decided to focus more on sharing actionable advice."

- **Track Lead Generation**: Social media is a great way to generate leads. Keep track of how many new connections or inquiries come from your posts, and follow up with any prospects who engage with your content.

Example: "After posting about how our CRM system helped a client streamline their processes, I received several messages from interested prospects who wanted to learn more."

- **Refine Your Strategy Over Time**: Don't be afraid to experiment with different types of content and posting schedules. Over time, you'll find what works best for your audience. Continuously refine your approach to ensure that your posts are having the desired impact.

Conclusion: Posting with Purpose

Posting on social media isn't just about broadcasting information—it's about building relationships, showcasing your expertise, and engaging with your audience in a meaningful way. By posting valuable content, engaging with others, and staying consistent, you can position yourself as a trusted expert in your field and attract the right opportunities.

Remember, posting is about quality, not quantity. Focus on adding value, fostering conversations, and staying active in your industry's online community. When done right, posting can be a powerful tool for driving sales, building your personal brand, and opening the door to new opportunities.

In the next chapter, we'll explore **Positioning**, where we'll discuss how to position yourself and your product or service in a way that resonates with your target audience and sets you apart from the competition.

CHAPTER 12: POSITIONING

Introduction: Why Positioning is Critical in Sales

Positioning is one of the most powerful tools you have in sales. It's the art of defining how you, your product, or your service fits into the minds of your prospects. Done well, it not only sets you apart from the competition but also ensures that your clients see you as the best possible solution to their needs.

Positioning isn't just about selling your product's features—it's about connecting those features to your client's specific pain points and showing how your solution fits into the bigger picture. In my own experience, the most successful salespeople are those who master the ability to position themselves and their product in a way that resonates with their target audience. When you do this effectively, prospects don't just see you as another option—they see you as the right choice.

In this chapter, we will look into how to position yourself, your product, or your service in a way that maximises its appeal to your prospects. We'll explore how to align your positioning with your clients' needs, how to differentiate yourself from the competition, and how to make sure your message cuts through the noise.

Step 1: Understand Your Client's Pain Points

The foundation of strong positioning is a deep understanding of your client's pain points. Before you can position yourself or your product effectively, you need to know what problems your prospects are facing and how your solution can help them. This requires research, asking the right questions, and truly listening to your client's needs.

I've always found that when I position my solution around the specific challenges my clients are dealing with, the conversation shifts from a sales pitch to a collaboration. Your clients don't want to be sold to—they want a partner who understands their problems and can offer a solution that fits seamlessly into their world.

Here's how to understand and address your client's pain points:

- **Research Your Client's Industry**: Take the time to understand the specific challenges facing your client's industry. What trends are shaping their business? What pressures are they under? This gives you valuable context for your conversations and helps you tailor your positioning to fit their situation.

Example: "If I'm working with a company in the retail sector, I know they might be facing challenges around supply chain disruptions or adapting to e-commerce growth. I position my solution as a way to improve operational efficiency and drive online sales."

- **Ask Open-Ended Questions**: During your conversations with prospects, ask open-ended questions that encourage them to talk about their challenges. This not only helps you uncover their pain points but also allows them to feel heard, which builds trust.

Example: "Can you tell me about the biggest challenge your team is facing right now? How is that impacting your overall business goals?"

- **Listen and Respond with Relevance**: Once you understand their pain points, tailor your message to show how your solution addresses those specific issues. Don't just talk about features—focus on how those features solve the problems your client cares about most.

Example: "Based on what you've shared, it sounds like improving customer retention is one of your top priorities. Our CRM tool is designed to help you engage customers more effectively by automating follow-ups and providing real-time insights into their behaviour."

Step 2: Differentiate Yourself from the Competition

In today's crowded marketplace, standing out from the competition is more important than ever.

If you don't differentiate yourself, your product, or your service, your prospects are likely to see you as just another option, making it harder to win the deal. Positioning is about finding your unique value proposition—what sets you apart and makes you the best choice.

I've always believed that differentiation doesn't mean you have to be radically different from everyone else. Sometimes, it's about highlighting subtle distinctions—things that might seem small but make a big difference to your clients. Whether it's a unique feature, exceptional customer service, or an in-depth understanding of your client's business, finding and communicating what sets you apart is key to winning more deals.

Here's how to differentiate yourself:

- **Identify Your Unique Value Proposition**: What makes you different from your competitors? Maybe it's a feature your product has that others don't, or maybe it's the personalised service you provide. Whatever it is, make sure you highlight it when positioning your solution.

Example: "While many CRM systems offer basic reporting, our tool goes a step further by providing predictive analytics that help you anticipate customer needs before they arise."

- **Focus on Value, Not Features**: Rather than getting bogged down in the technical details of what your product does, focus on the value it brings to your client. What outcomes can they expect? How will it improve their business or solve their specific problems?

Example: "We're not just offering a CRM system—we're offering a tool that will help you retain more customers, increase engagement, and ultimately drive more revenue."

- **Leverage Client Success Stories**: Sharing stories of how you've helped other clients succeed is a great way to differentiate yourself. These stories show prospects that you don't just talk the talk—you've helped businesses like theirs achieve real results.

Example: "One of our clients in the same industry increased their sales by 15% after implementing our solution. I'd be happy to share the details of how we worked with them to make that happen."

Step 3: Align Your Positioning with Your Client's Goals

Strong positioning is not just about highlighting your product's strengths—it's about aligning those strengths with your client's specific goals. The more your message speaks to what your client is trying to achieve, the more likely they are to see your solution as a perfect fit.

I always remind the salespeople I train that positioning is about creating a connection between what you offer and what the client needs. This requires listening closely to their goals and objectives, and then positioning your solution as a tool that will help them reach those goals.

Here's how to align your positioning with your client's goals:

- **Understand Their Business Objectives**: Take the time to learn about your client's overall business goals. Are they trying to grow revenue? Improve efficiency? Expand into new markets? Once you understand their objectives, you can position your product or service as a key part of their strategy.

Example: "If a client's goal is to grow their customer base, I position our CRM system as a tool that will help them manage leads more effectively and nurture prospects into long-term customers."

- **Tailor Your Message**: Generic messaging doesn't work when it comes to positioning. Tailor your pitch to show how your product helps your client meet their specific objectives. The more closely your message aligns with their goals, the stronger your positioning will be.

Example: "You mentioned that increasing customer satisfaction is a top priority for your team. Our solution will help you achieve that by providing tools that make it easier to track customer feedback and address issues before they escalate."

- **Be Specific About Outcomes**: Clients want to know exactly how your solution will help them achieve their goals. Be specific about the outcomes they can expect from using your product or service, and quantify those benefits whenever possible.

Example: "By using our system, you can expect to see a 20% reduction in customer churn over the next six months, helping you retain more customers and boost your bottom line."

Step 4: Use "We" Language to Position Yourself as a Team Player

As we discussed in the earlier chapter on perception, using "we" instead of "I" helps create the perception that you're part of a bigger organisation. But it also does something equally important: it positions you as a team player who is invested in the client's success.

When you use "we" language, you're positioning yourself as a partner who is working alongside the client to achieve their goals, rather than as someone who is simply selling them a product. This collaborative approach builds trust and makes clients feel like you're invested in their success, which can make all the difference in winning the deal.

Here's how to position yourself as a partner:

- **Use "We" Instead of "I"**: This subtle shift in language can make a big difference in how you're perceived. Instead of saying "I will help you achieve this," say "We will work together to make this happen." It positions you as a partner, not just a vendor.

Example: "We'll work closely with your team to ensure that the system is fully integrated and that you see results within the first three months."

- **Highlight Your Support Team**: Even if you're a solo operator, talk about the team behind you. Whether it's a customer support team, product developers, or external partners, emphasising that you have a broader support network reassures the client that they're in good hands.

Example: "Our dedicated support team will be there every step of the way to help with onboarding and training, ensuring a smooth transition for your team."

- **Focus on Collaboration**: Position your solution as something that you'll implement together with the client. Emphasise the collaborative nature of your work and frame the sales process as a partnership.

Example: "We'll collaborate with your team to tailor the system to your specific workflows, ensuring it's fully aligned with how your business operates."

Step 5: Stay Agile and Adapt Your Positioning Over Time

Positioning isn't something you do once and then forget about. It's an ongoing process that requires flexibility and adaptation. As your client's needs evolve, as your industry changes, and as new competitors enter the market, you'll need to refine your positioning to stay relevant and continue to stand out.

I've always approached positioning as a dynamic, flexible process. Just as the sales landscape shifts, so too should your positioning strategy. By staying agile and adapting your positioning over time, you can ensure that you remain a top choice for your clients, no matter how the market evolves. Here's how to stay agile with your positioning:

- **Monitor Industry Trends**: Stay on top of trends and changes in your client's industry. If new challenges or opportunities arise, adjust your positioning to show how your solution is uniquely suited to address those changes.

Example: "As remote work continues to grow, our CRM system is designed to help distributed teams stay connected and manage customer relationships seamlessly, no matter where they are."

- **Listen to Client Feedback**: Your clients are a valuable source of feedback on your positioning.

If you notice that certain aspects of your message aren't resonating, or if clients are consistently raising the same objections, use that feedback to refine your positioning.

Example: "I noticed that clients were hesitant about the complexity of our solution, so I started positioning it as a user-friendly, intuitive tool that doesn't require a steep learning curve."

- **Test and Adjust**: Don't be afraid to experiment with different positioning messages to see what resonates best with your clients. Test different approaches, track the results, and adjust accordingly.

Conclusion: Positioning Yourself for Success

Positioning is the key to standing out in a crowded marketplace and ensuring that your clients see you as the best solution to their needs. By understanding your client's pain points, differentiating yourself from the competition, aligning your message with their goals, and positioning yourself as a partner, you create a powerful narrative that resonates with your prospects.

Remember, positioning is an ongoing process. Stay agile, listen to feedback, and continuously refine your message to stay relevant and compelling in your industry.

In the next chapter, we'll discuss **Perseverance**, where we'll explore how to stay motivated, consistent, and resilient in the face of challenges as you work toward long-term sales success.

Conclusion: Putting the 'P's Together for Sales Success

The methods and principles discussed throughout this book are not isolated tactics but interconnected elements of a successful sales strategy. Together, they form a holistic approach to sales that is thoughtful, strategic, and client focused.

By mastering each of these "P"s, you'll not only improve your chances of closing deals, but you'll also build stronger relationships, establish yourself as an expert in your field, and create lasting success. Sales is not about forcing a product on someone—it's about helping clients find solutions to their problems, educating them, and being there for them in the long run.

I hope the strategies in this book have given you a new perspective on the sales process and empowered you to approach it with confidence. With the right mindset, preparation, and perseverance, you'll find that success in sales is not about pushing—it's about aligning with your clients' needs and building trust through meaningful, thoughtful engagement.

Now, it's time to take what you've learned and put it into action. Remember, every interaction is an opportunity to improve, to build relationships, and to make a lasting impact. Keep refining your approach, stay true to your purpose, and above all, enjoy the process.

Thank you for joining me on this journey of **Taking the P Out of Sales**. Here's to your continued success in the world of sales!

Printed in Great Britain
by Amazon